The **ESSEI** of
Accounting II

Duane R. Milano, Ph.D.
Professor of Accounting
East Texas State University, Commerce, TX

Charles S. Robnett, M.B.A.
East Texas State University, Commerce, TX

Research & Education Association
Visit our website at
www.rea.com

Research & Education Association
61 Ethel Road West
Piscataway, New Jersey 08854
E-mail: info@rea.com

THE ESSENTIALS®
OF ACCOUNTING II

Year 2006 Printing

Printed in the United States of America

Library of Congress Control Number 99-74562

International Standard Book Number 0-87891-672-5

What REA's Essentials®
Will Do for You

This book is part of REA's celebrated *Essentials*® series of review and study guides, relied on by tens of thousands of students over the years for being complete yet concise.

Here you'll find a summary of the very material you're most likely to need for exams, not to mention homework— eliminating the need to read and review many pages of textbook and class notes.

This slim volume condenses the vast amount of detail characteristic of the subject matter and summarizes the **essentials** of the field. The book provides quick access to the important facts, principles, theorems, concepts, and equations in the field.

It will save you hours of study and preparation time.

This *Essentials*® book has been prepared by experts in the field and has been carefully reviewed to ensure its accuracy and maximum usefulness. We believe you'll find it a valuable, handy addition to your library.

Larry B. Kling
Chief Editor

CONTENTS

This book is a continuation of "*THE ESSENTIALS OF ACCOUNTING I*" and begins with Chapter 13. It covers the usual course outline of Accounting II. Earlier/related topics are covered in "*THE ESSENTIALS OF ACCOUNTING I.*"

CHAPTER 13

CURRENT LIABILITIES

13.1 CURRENT LIABILITIES DEFINED

Current liabilities are those obligations which must be paid within one year. This includes the portion of long-term debt that is due and payable within one year. Common types of current liabilities include accounts payable, notes payable, accrued liabilities for wages or interest as well as estimated liabilities such as income taxes.

13.2 ACCOUNTS PAYABLE

Accounts payable arise when a business purchases inventory or equipment on a credit basis. An example of the journal entry to reflect the purchase of inventory on credit is shown in Example 13.2.1.

EXAMPLE 13.2.1

The Sample Company
General Journal

Date	Description	Debit	Credit

	Purchases	10,000	
	Accounts Payable		10,000

The use of the purchases account is limited strictly to purchases of **inventory** on credit. Purchases of other items would be reflected as affecting those accounts directly. As an example, if equipment were purchased on account, the journal entry to reflect that is shown in Example 13.2.2.

EXAMPLE 13.2.2

The Sample Company
General Journal

Date	Description	Debit	Credit
	Equipment	5,000	
	Accounts Payable		5,000

Payment of those payables are recorded as a debit to accounts payable and a credit to cash as shown in Example 13.2.3.

EXAMPLE 13.2.3

The Sample Company
General Journal

Date	Description	Debit	Credit
	Accounts Payable	5,000	
	Cash		5,000

13.3 NOTES PAYABLE

Notes payable occur when a business borrows money. Business transactions such as the purchase of real estate or equipment, as well as a temporary need for additional working capital, may necessitate such borrowings. As an example, assume that on March 15, 1999, Smith Corporation borrows $100,000 from its bank for 90 days. Interest is payable at maturity and accrues as a rate of 12%. The journal entry to record this transaction is shown in Example 13.3.1.

EXAMPLE 13.3.1

The Sample Company
General Journal

Date	Description	Debit	Credit
1999 Mr15	Cash	100,000	
	Notes Payable		100,000

On June 15, 1999, Smith Corporation repaid the loan plus $3,000 interest ($100,000 x 12% x 90/360). In this instance, a 360-day year is used for interest calculation. The journal entry to record this transaction is shown in Example 13.3.2.

EXAMPLE 13.3.2

The Sample Company
General Journal

Date	Description	Debit	Credit
1999 Jn15	Notes Payable	100,000	
	Interest Expense	3,000	
	Cash		103,000

13.4   LIABILITY FOR SALARIES AND WAGES

Employees are rarely paid on a daily basis. Instead, a business **accrues** liability for payroll between pay dates (usually bi-weekly). The gross amount of **wages** is relatively easy to calculate, consisting of hours worked multiplied by the hourly wage. **Salaries** are paid bi-weekly or monthly based on some present annual amount. Employers are also responsible for withholding a portion of gross pay for social security (FICA) and Federal income taxes. In addition, the employer may withhold State and municipal income taxes (if applicable). Example 13.4.1 reflects the journal entry necessary to record payroll expense and liabilities as of January 15, 1999 (the end of the payroll period).

EXAMPLE 13.4.1

The Sample Company
General Journal

Date	Description	Debit	Credit
1999 Ja15	Sales Salaries Expense	10,000	
	Office Wages Expense	5,000	
	FICA Tax Payable		1,050
	Liability for Income Tax Withheld		2,500
	Accrued Payroll		11,450

In this example, although the business has incurred $15,000 in total salary and wages expenses, only $11,450 is actually paid out to employees. The remainder will be submitted to the appropriate government agency at regular intervals. Other withholdings, such as union dues, would be handled similarly.

At the same time, an employer incurs liabilities for certain payroll taxes. These include FICA tax (figured at the same rate and on the same amount of earnings as the employees), Federal unemployment tax, and State unemployment tax. The journal entry to record the employer's tax expense and liabilities is reflected in Example 13.4.2.

EXAMPLE 13.4.2

The Sample Company
General Journal

Date	Description	Debit	Credit
1999 Ja15	Payroll Tax Expense	2,790	
	FICA Tax Payable		1,050
	State Unemployment Tax Payable		810
	Federal Unemployment Tax Payable		930

13.5 WARRANTIES

A business may have liabilities that, while quite real, can only be estimated. A company which sells appliances with warranties can incur this kind of liability. In such situations, the company guarantees free repair within a specified period of time in the event of a problem with their product.

The estimate of the probable expense of such repairs may be based on prior experience. In such a case, the liability for warranties might be a percentage of total sales in a given period. For example, assume the Sample Company sells 200 refrigerators in 1992 with one year warranties. Based on past experience, the company expects 5% of its refrigerators to be defective within the one year warranty period. The average service call is estimated at $25. During 1992, 3 refrigerators are repaired at a total cost of $70. In 1993, 6 refrigerators are repaired at a cost of $130. Example 13.5.1 reflects the entries necessary to record expenditures for repairs as well as the entry to estimate warranty liability. Note that warranty **expense** is incurred in the accounting period when the refrigerators are sold, not when the repairs are made.

EXAMPLE 13.5.1

Date	Description	Debit	Credit
1992 Various	Warranty Expense Cash, Parts, Labor	70	70

To record $70 repair costs in 1989

Date	Description	Debit	Credit
Dec 31	Warranty Expense Estimated Liability Under Warranty Obligations	175	175

To record estimated liability under warranties for repairs to be performed on refrigerators sold in 1992. Two hundred (200) refrigerators sold x .05 = 10 estimated to need repair. 10 – 3 repaired in 1992 = 7 estimated to be repaired in 1993 at $25 each for estimated liability of $175.

Example 13.5.2 illustrates the entries to record the cost of warranty repairs during 1993.

EXAMPLE 13.5.2

Date	Description	Debit	Credit
1993 Various	Estimated Liability Under Warranty Obligations Cash, Parts, Labor	130	130

To record expenditures related to 1992 sales.

At the end of 1993, the Estimated Liability Under Warranty Obligations account will show a $45 credit balance. Ideally, the balance in this account would be zero if the company's estimate had been perfect. Since the estimating process is an ongoing one, there is no need to adjust the liability account unless it becomes obvious that the estimates are continually too high or too low. In such cases, a revision of the firm's estimating process is warranted.

13.6   RETURNABLE DEPOSITS

Businesses may sometimes require customers to put up cash deposits as part of a business transaction. For example, an apartment owner may require a renter to put up a deposit equivalent to two month's rent. This deposit is usually refundable to the renter under certain conditions specified in the rental contract. Since the apartment owner is obligated to return the deposit if the contract terms are met, this amount is a liability of the company. Example 13.6.1 illustrates such a situation.

Assume that a renter is required to put up a $500 deposit upon renting an apartment on May 1, 1992. On May 1, 1993, the renter moves out after meeting all provisions of the rental contract. The entries to record those events are shown below.

EXAMPLE 13.6.1

Date	Description	Debit	Credit
1992 May 1	Cash Returnable Deposits	500	500

To record receipt of $500 apartment deposit.

1993 May 1	Returnable Deposits Cash	500	500

To record refund of $500 apartment deposit.

CHAPTER 14

LONG-TERM LIABILITIES

14.1 DEFINITIONS

Long-term liabilities are liabilities that have an expected life of more than one year. Usually a long-term liability will be reclassified as current near the end of its life. In other cases, the life of the liability may not be clearly known. In these cases, the classification is done on the best estimate of the expected life; current if less than one year and long-term if more than one year.

Three types of liabilities that could conceivably be long-term are notes payable, product warranties and returnable deposits. These items were covered in Chapter 13. It should be noted that often notes payable will be long-term upon the signing of the notes.

The topic that takes up the majority of discussion about long-term liabilities is **bonds payable**. This topic is covered in Chapter 15 along with the asset side of bonds.

14.2 PENSIONS

During recent years, **pensions** have become a much more

involved and debated topic. This is a result of numerous factors. In 1974, Congress passed the Employee Retirement Income Security Act (**ERISA**) which set up special rules for protecting employee benefits. Under these guidelines, a pension plan can be either **contributory** or **noncontributory, qualified** or **unqualified,** and **funded** or **unfunded.** Each of these distinctions will be examined individually.

It has become increasingly difficult for organizations to set up qualified plans and follow all of the law's requirements. Most companies now get expert legal and accounting assistance to assure compliance.

14.2.1 CONTRIBUTORY AND NONCONTRIBUTORY

A **contributory plan** provides that the employer withholds a portion of the employee's earnings as a contribution to the pension. The employer also contributes a portion as specified in the plan.

Under a **noncontributory plan**, the employer incurs the entire burden of the plan. The employees do not make a contribution.

14.2.2 QUALIFIED OR UNQUALIFIED

A **qualified plan** is one that complies with the federal income tax requirements which allow the deduction of the pension contributions on the income tax returns of the employer. Most plans are qualified. It would be much to the disadvantage for all concerned if an unqualified plan were set up. To the employer, the contributions would not be a tax expense. As a result of that, the employer will be likely to pass this cost on to the employees in the form of lower compensation.

14.2.3 FUNDED AND UNFUNDED

A **funded plan** is one in which the employer makes pension payments to an independent funding agency. This agency is then responsible for accounting for all contributions to and disbursements from the fund. The most common independent funding agencies are insurance companies. An **unfunded plan** is managed completely by the employer rather than an independent agency.

14.2.4 NET PERIODIC PENSION COST

For any given year, the employer's cost of an employee's pension plan is called the **net periodic pension cost**. This cost is charged to the operating expense account called **Pension Expense**. The credit will be totally to cash if it is a fully funded plan. If it is partially funded, any unfunded portion will be credited to an account called **Unfunded Pension Cost**. A sample entry is given in Example 14.2.4.

EXAMPLE 14.2.4

The Sample Company
General Journal

Date	Acct. No.	Description	Debit	Credit
1992 Dec31	27	Pension Expenses	12,000	
	1	Cash		5,000
	12	Unfunded Pension – Accrued Costs		7,000

To record the 1992 funding of pension plan.

Depending on when the unfunded portion is to be paid, this account can be either a current liability or a long-term liability.

The employer's financial statements should very clearly state all pertinent details of the pension plan. These would include who is covered, how the plan is funded, what sort of accounting is done for the plan, and other details deemed essential to understanding the plan.

14.3 CONTINGENT LIABILITIES

Potential obligations that will result only if certain future events occur are called **contingent liabilities**. If the amount is definite then it should be noted. More likely, a contingent liability is for an indefinite amount.

Examples would be lawsuits that are being settled in court, and notes that are guaranteed by the company. The company would only have to pay if the originator of the notes did not pay them.

Contingent liabilities can be shown in the balance sheet between long-term liabilities and stockholders' equity. However, they do not need to be detailed in the body of the balance sheet. Instead they can be disclosed in footnotes to the financial statements. In the increasingly litigation-happy mood of the United States, contingent liabilities have taken on an increasingly important role in financial statements.

14.4 UNEARNED REVENUE (DEFERRALS)

Revenue that is collected in advance of earning it is called **unearned revenue**. It is also sometimes referred to as **revenue collected in advance**. When the revenue is first collected, the entry would be as in Example 14.4.1.

EXAMPLE 14.4.1

The Sample Company
General Journal

Date	Acct. No.	Description	Debit	Credit
1992 Jan 1	4	Accounts Receivable: Smith Company	3,000	
	17	Unearned Sales Rev.		3,000

To record revenue collected in advance from Smith Company.

Examples of such collections in advance might be airline tickets paid for in advance, advertising, or insurance premiums. Another large category would be repairs paid for in advance such as service contracts. As the revenue is earned the journal entry would be made as in Example 14.4.2.

EXAMPLE 14.4.2

The Sample Company
General Journal

Date	Acct. No.	Description	Debit	Credit
1993 Jan 1	17	Unearned Sales Revenue	1,000	
	60	Sales Revenue		1,000

To record sales of merchandise that was paid for in advance.

Unearned revenue is usually shown on the balance sheet as a current liability. This placement would, however, depend on the length of time involved. It is very likely that this would be a long-term liability.

CHAPTER 15

BONDS

15.1 BONDS DEFINED

A corporation may seek long-term financing through the issuance of **bonds**. Bonds are similar to notes payable in that the corporation is obligated to repay a stated amount at a specific time and to pay interest at regular intervals to investors. There is, however, an important difference. Notes payable are usually owed to one investor, but bonds can be subdivided and sold to many investors through securities brokers. This allows a corporation to raise larger amounts of money than might be obtainable from any single lender. While bonds are traded as marketable securities, they differ from stock in that bonds are debt instruments only. Ownership of a bond does not provide an ownership interest in the issuing entity.

15.2 PURCHASE OF BONDS

A corporation may purchase bonds of another entity as an investment. The journal entry to record the purchase of a bond may involve accounting for accrued interest if the purchase date is between bond interest payment dates. Assume, for example, on August 1, 1999, an investor purchases a $100,000 Smith Corporation bond at face value. The bond pays 12% interest semi-annually on June 1st and December 1st. The journal entry to record this purchase is shown in Example 15.2.1.

EXAMPLE 15.2.1

Date	Description	Debit	Credit
1999 Aug 1	Marketable Securities Bond Interest Receivable Cash	100,000 2,000	 102,000

The $2,000 debit to bond interest receivable consists of interest accrued during the 60 day period between the last interest date (June 1st) and the purchase date (August 1st). This amount (calculated as $100,000 x .12 x 60/360), is added to the purchase price of the bonds ($100,000) for a total cash outlay of $102,000. The investor will recover the $2,000 when the regular interest payment is received at the next interest date.

15.3 INCOME ON BONDS RECEIVABLE

Using the previous example, on December 1st, the investor will receive interest of $6,000 (calculated as $100,000 x .12 x 180/360) for the six months ending December 1st. The journal entry to record this transaction is shown in Example 15.3.1.

EXAMPLE 15.3.1

Date	Description	Debit	Credit
1999 Dec1 1999	Cash Bond Interest Receivable Bond Interest Revenue	6,000	 2,000 4,000

Only the portion earned since the purchase of the bonds on August 1st is recognized as revenue.

Again using the same example, if the investor maintains calendar year records, bond interest accrued from the December 1 payment date should be accounted for as shown in Example 15.3.2.

EXAMPLE 15.3.2

Date	Description	Debit	Credit
1999 Dec 31	Bond Interest Receivable Bond Interest Revenue	1,000	1,000

This journal entry recognizes that interest revenue has been earned since the last payment date (December 1), but has not yet been received. Example 15.3.3 reflects the journal entry to record the receipt of the next regular interest payment of $6,000 on June 1, 2000. In this example, the revenue earned during this period (January 1 to June 1) is recognized as revenue and the bond interest receivable account created at year-end is paid off.

EXAMPLE 15.3.3

Date	Description	Debit	Credit
2000 Jun 1	Cash Bond Interest Receivable Bond Interest Revenue	6,000	1,000 5,000

15.4   BONDS PAYABLE

A corporation may choose to raise funds through the issuance of bonds, which become long-term liabilities of the business. As an example, assume a corporation intends to raise $1,000,000 by selling bonds that carry a 12% interest rate, payable semi-annually on July 1st and January 1st. If these bonds can be sold at face value on July 1st, the journal entry is shown in Example 15.4.1.

EXAMPLE 15.4.1

Date	Description	Debit	Credit
1999 Jul 1	Cash Bonds Payable	1,000,000	1,000,000

The journal entry to record the semi-annual interest payments each January 1st and July 1st is shown in Example 15.4.2. The semi-annual interest payment of $60,000 is calculated as $1,000,000 x .12 x 180/360.

EXAMPLE 15.4.2

Date	Description	Debit	Credit
	Bond Interest Expense Cash	60,000	60,000

At maturity, the necessary entry to record redemption of the bonds is shown in Example 15.4.3.

EXAMPLE 15.4.3

Date	Description	Debit	Credit
	Bonds Payable Cash	1,000,000	1,000,000

If the bonds were issued between interest dates, for example on April 1st, the purchase cost would include the interest accrued during the 90 day period between the last interest payment date (January 1) and the purchase date (April 1). This accrued interest, calculated as $1,000,000 \times .12 \times 90/360$, is reflected as a liability account called Bond Interest Payable. Example 15.4.4 shows the entry needed in such an event.

EXAMPLE 15.4.4

Date	Description	Debit	Credit
1999 Apr1	Cash	1,030,000	
	Bonds Payable		1,000,000
	Bond Interest Payable		30,000

At the next regular payment date (July 1), the corporation will pay bondholders the full amount of interest earned since the last payment date (January 1). As shown in Example 15.4.5, only the amount of interest accruing from the issue date of April 1 is recognized as an expense.

EXAMPLE 15.4.5

Date	Description	Debit	Credit
1999 Jul 1	Bond Interest Payable	30,000	
	Bond Interest Expense	30,000	
	Cash		60,000

15.5   BOND ISSUE PRICE

Previous examples have assumed issue of bonds at face (par)

value. The issue price of bonds often differs from face value due to two factors: (1) The relationship between the bond interest rate and the market rate required by investors; and (2) The perceived ability of the issuing entity to pay the interest and principal required by the bond terms.

15.6 BONDS SOLD AT A DISCOUNT

If a corporation issues bonds paying 8%, but investors require a 10% return, the bond issue price will be less than the face amount. Investors are thus discounting the bonds' value to a point where the combined yield of interest income plus the difference in purchase price and the face amount is equivalent to a 10% yield over the life of the bond. Example 15.6.1 reflects a situation where a $1,000,000 bond issue with a 10 year maturity is sold for $950,000. The difference between the face value and the actual sales price is the discount.

EXAMPLE 15.6.1

Date	Description	Debit	Credit
	Cash Discounts on Bonds Payable Bonds Payable	950,000 50,000	 1,000,000

The discount must be amortized over the life of the bond. The simplest method of amortization is the straight-line method, allocating an equal portion of the discount to bond interest expense at each interest payment date. Amortization of the $50,000 discount ($50,000/10 years = $5,000 annually or $2,500 semi-annually) and payment of interest ($1,000,000 x .08 x 180/ 360 = $40,000 semi-annually) are shown in Example 15.6.2.

EXAMPLE 15.6.2

Date	Description	Debit	Credit
	Bond Interest Expense Cash	40,000	40,000
	Bond Interest Expense Bond Discount	2,500	2,500

15.7 BONDS SOLD AT A PREMIUM

If the rate of interest paid on a bond exceeds the market rate, investors will pay a premium over the face amount. Using the previous example of a $1,000,000 bond issue, but changing the bond interest rate to 12% (the market rate remains 10%), the bonds may sell for $1,050,000. Example 15.7.1 reflects the effect of this transaction.

EXAMPLE 15.7.1

Date	Description	Debit	Credit
	Cash Bonds Payable Premium on Bonds Payable	1,050,000	1,000,000 50,000

Like the bond discount, the bond premium must be amortized over the life of the bond. The semi-annual journal entry to record the required interest payment plus the premium amortization is shown in Example 15.7.2.

EXAMPLE 15.7.2

Date	Description	Debit	Credit
	Bond Interest Expense Cash	60,000	60,000
	Premium on Bonds Payable Bond Interest Expense	2,500	2,500

Should interest payment dates not coincide with period-end, the interest accrued since the last payment date must be recognized. Using the above example, but changing the interest payment dates to June 1st and December 1st, the entry required at year-end is shown in Example 15.7.3. One month's interest $1,000,000 x .12 x 30/360) is $10,000 while one month's premium amortization is $417 ($50,000/10 = $5,000 annually or $417 per month).

EXAMPLE 15.7.3

Date	Description	Debit	Credit
Dec 1	Bond Interest Expense Bond Interest Payable	10,000	10,000
	Premium on Bonds Payable Bond Interest Expense	417	417

The entry then required at the next regular interest payment date of June 1st is shown in Example 15.7.4.

This properly recognizes only the expenses incurred during this accounting period.

EXAMPLE 15.7.4

Date	Description	Debit	Credit
Jun 1	Bond Interest Payable Bond Interest Expense Premium on Bonds Payable Cash	10,000 47,917 2,083	 60,000

15.8 EFFECTIVE INTEREST METHOD

Previous examples have assumed the use of straight-line amortization of bond discount or premium. While simple to calculate, the Accounting Principles Board has ruled that the straight-line method should be used only if its use does not result in a material difference from the **effective interest method**. The weakness in the straight-line method is the fact that bond interest expense is the same each period, while the carrying value of the bond increases (if amortizing a discount) or decreases (if amortizing a premium) each period. In such cases, the **effective interest rate** for the bonds varies each period.

Use of the effective interest method provides a steady rate of interest expense over the life of the bond. Interest expense each period is calculated as the **market rate** at the time of issue times the carrying value of the bonds (defined as face value minus unamortized discount or plus unamortized premium).

Like the previous example 15.7.1, in which the market rate of interest was 10% (compared to an actual interest of 12% on the bonds), assume bonds with a face value of $1,000,000 were sold for $1,077,217 creating a premium of $77,217 to be amortized over the life of the bonds (five years in this example). As shown

EXAMPLE 15.8.1

Face value of bonds = $1,000,000
Stated rate of interest: 0.12
Market rate of interest 0.10
Life of bonds = 5 years

Semi-annual Interest Period	Carrying Value at Beginning of Period	Semi-annual Interest Expense	Semi-annual Interest Paid	Amortization of Premium	Unamortized Bond Premium at End of Period	Carrying Value at End of Period
0					77,217	1,077,217
1	1,077,217	53,861	60,000	6,139	71,078	1,071,078
2	1,071,078	53,554	60,000	6,446	64,632	1,064,632
3	1,064,632	53,232	60,000	6,768	57,864	1,057,864
4	1,057,864	52,893	60,000	7,107	50,757	1,050,757
5	1,050,757	52,538	60,000	7,462	43,295	1,043,295
6	1,043,295	52,165	60,000	7,835	35,460	1,035,460
7	1,035,460	51,773	60,000	8,227	27,232	1,027,232
8	1,027,232	51,362	60,000	8,638	18,594	1,018,594
9	1,018,594	50,930	60,000	9,070	9,524	1,009,524
10	1,009,524	50,476	60,000	9,524	0	1,000,000

in Example 15.8.1, semi-annual interest expense is calculated based on the **market rate**, not the face rate. Carrying value at the end of the period is calculated as carrying value at the beginning of the period less premium amortization for that period. Note that the carrying value is equal to the face value at the end of semi-annual period 10 (maturity of the bonds).

15.9   RETIREMENT OF BONDS PAYABLE

Bonds may include provision for redemption at the issuer's option for a specified price. In any event, a corporation may redeem its bonds by purchasing them in the open market. If the purchase price is less than the carrying value, a gain is realized on retirement of the debt. If the price is higher than the carrying value, a loss is realized. For example, assume a corporation intends to purchase $500,000 of its own bonds at a price of 102 (102% of face value), or $510,000. Also assume the bonds have an unamortized premium of $5,000. The journal entry to record this transaction is shown in Example 15.9.1.

EXAMPLE 15.9.1

Date	Description	Debit	Credit
	Bonds Payable	500,000	
	Premium on Bonds Payable	5,000	
	Loss on Redemption of Bonds	5,000	
	Cash		510,000

Conversely, if the bonds can be purchased at 98 (98% of face value), or $490,000, the necessary journal entry is shown in Example 15.9.2.

EXAMPLE 15.9.2

Date	Description	Debit	Credit
	Bonds Payable	500,000	
	Premium on Bonds Payable	5,000	
	Gain on Redemption of		
	Bonds		15,000
	Cash		490,000

CHAPTER 16

PARTNERSHIPS

16.1.1 CHARACTERISTICS OF PARTNERSHIPS

As defined by the Uniform Partnership Act, a **partnership** is the combination of two or more people for the purpose of co-owning a business for profit. A partnership is basically a form of business between the sole proprietorship and a corporation.

There are a number of distinctive characteristics about partnerships. They include life of partnership, mutual agency, participation in income, as well as many others. We will look at a number of these in the following sections of this chapter.

16.1.2 LIMITED LIFE

The **life of a partnership** is limited. This is because a partnership is dissolved if any of the partners leave the firm. Possible reasons include death of a partner, withdrawal of a partner and bankruptcy. A new partnership must also be started if a new partner is admitted.

16.1.3 UNLIMITED LIABILITY

The usual form of a partnership is a **general partnership** where all partners have **unlimited liability**. That is, when a partnership is found to be insolvent, for whatever reason, the partners must contribute enough of their own personal assets to resolve the insolvency.

There is a form of partnership, **limited partnership**, where the limited partners are liable only to the level of their investment in the partnership. However, all partnerships must have at least one general partner who will have unlimited liability.

16.1.4 CO-OWNERSHIP OF PROPERTY

All property in a partnership is owned by all partners. In the case of a dissolution, partner claims to assets will be determined by their capital account balances.

16.1.5 MUTUAL AGENCY

Mutual agency means that any one partner can make a deal on behalf of the partnership. All other partners are then legally bound by such agreements.

16.1.6 PARTICIPATION IN INCOME

All partners have **participation of income** in the partnership. Losses and income are both distributed according to the partnership agreement. If the agreement is silent to the level of participation, then all partners share equally.

If the partnership agreement does not speak to the issue of losses, they are distributed on the same basis as income.

16.1.7 NONTAXABLE ENTITY

A partnership is a **nontaxable entity**. It is therefore, not required to pay taxes. It does nevertheless, file forms with the IRS that give details about partnership operations. These are called **Information forms.**

16.2 ADVANTAGES AND DISADVANTAGES OF PARTNERSHIP

A partnership is very **easy to set up** and begin. It also provides for **Increased managerial skills** – those of the additional partners. It is easier to raise capital than in a sole proprietorship. Often the partners will be **taxed at a lower rate** than if the organization was a corporation and was a taxed entity.

At the same time there can be major disadvantages to a partnership. These include most of the characteristics of a partnership; co-ownership of property, mutual agency, limited life, and unlimited liability. It is also usually more difficult to raise capital with a partnership than a corporation.

16.3 ACCOUNTING FOR PARTNERSHIPS

Most of the accounting for partnerships will be identical with that for businesses run by individuals that we have discussed in earlier chapters. The chart of accounts can be identical except for **drawing** and **capital** accounts for each partner.

The main areas of differences in accounting for partnerships is formation, liquidation and income distribution. We will next look at many of these unique accounting techniques.

16.4 ACCOUNTING FOR INVESTMENTS IN PARTNERSHIP

An individual entry will be made for each partner's contribution to the partnership. Any assets and liabilities turned over to the partnership will be debited and credited as they normally would.

The partner's capital is credited for the net amount.

For instance, assume that two sole proprietorships involved in servicing microcomputers are going to be merged into a partnership. Each of the partners is to contribute various assets (including some cash from both) and liabilities to the partnership. The entry for recording the contributions of Jimmie Techie is illustrated in Example 16.4.1.

EXAMPLE 16.4.1

The Sample Partnership
General Journal

Date	Acct. No.	Description	Debit	Credit
1992				
Jan15	1	Cash	2,000	
	3	Accounts Receivable	4,000	
	11	Merchandise Inventory	4,500	
	15	Office Equipment	3,500	
	4	Allowance for Doubtful Accounts		800
	23	Accounts Payable		2,500
	31	Jimmie Techie – Capital		10,700

To record the investment of Jimmie Techie in the partnership.

Note that all the assets contributed by Jimmie equaled a total of $14,000. When taking account the Allowance for Doubtful Accounts Receivable, and the Accounts Payable, the net contribution for Jimmie will be $10,700:

$2,000+$4,000+$4,500+$3,500-$800-$2,500 = $10,700$

A similar entry would be done for each partner admitted to the partnership. In each case the partner would have a capital account with their name.

16.5   PARTNERSHIP INCOME DIVISION

There are three basic ways to divide income of a partnership. One is to do a simple division of income (or loss) on the **basis of a percentage to each partner**. Another method would be to recognize **service of partners**. The last method would be to recognize the **service and investment of partners**. Of course any combination of these three could also be used.

The important point to remember is that the division of income (or loss) is on the basis of the partnership agreement. If the agreement does not speak to the issue of division, then we assume it is equal amount for all partners.

For purposes of demonstrating the various methods, assume the information in Table 16.5.1 was provided.

TABLE 16.5.1

SAMPLE PARTNERSHIP
Accounting Information on Partners

Explanation	Techie	Softie	Total
Capital Account	30,000	40,000	70,000
Salary	30,000	20,000	50,000

16.5.1 STRAIGHT DIVISION OF INCOME

The most common basis for splitting income and loss in a partnership is by a **percentage formula** laid out in the partnership agreement. If the agreement specified that income is to be split in equal amounts for each partner, and there was net income of $35,000, the journal entry to record the division of income would be as in Example 16.5.1.

EXAMPLE 16.5.1

The Sample Partnership
General Journal

Date	Acct. No.	Description	Debit	Credit
1992 Dec31	40	Revenue and Expense Summary	35,000	
	31	Techie – Capital		17,500
	15	Softie – Capital		17,500

To record the division of 1992 income.

If there had been a loss instead of income, the Revenue and Expense Summary would have been credited for the amount of the loss, and each partner's capital account would be debited for one-half of the loss.

16.5.2 RECOGNIZING SERVICE OF PARTNERS

Often, a partnership agreement will call for a certain salary level for one or more of the partners. Let's assume the salary levels as given in Table 16.5. Also assume that there was an income of $40,000 for the year. Finally, we will assume that the agreement calls for equal division of income and is silent with respect to losses. The calculations of each partner's share is given in Table 16.5.2.

TABLE 16.5.2

Techie Salary	$30,000
Softie Salary	20,000
Total Salary	$50,000
Yearly Income	40,000
Excess of Allowances over Income	$10,000

This means that effectively, the partnership has a loss of $10,000 after salaries are paid. Each partner will then have a $5,000 loss. The income division is shown in Example 16.5.2.

EXAMPLE 16.5.2

The Sample Partnership
General Journal

Date	Acct. No.	Description	Debit	Credit
1992 Dec31	40	Revenue and Expense Summary	40,000	
	31	Techie – Capital		25,000
	15	Softie – Capital		15,000

To record the division of 1992 income.

If either of the partners had taken their money out in cash, the credit for their portion would have been to the cash in bank account.

16.5.3 RECOGNIZING SERVICE OF PARTNERS AND INVESTMENT

Often, a partnership agreement will call for recognition of the partners' investment, in addition to the salary allowances. This is usually done on an agreed upon interest rate which should be included in the partnership agreement.

Let's assume the salary levels as given in Table 16.5.2. Also assume that there was an income of $90,000 for the year, and that the agreement calls for equal division of income and is silent with respect to losses. Finally, assume that the agreement calls for an interest rate of 20 percent on investment. Table 16.5.3 shows the calculation of each partner's share.

TABLE 16.5.3

Techie Salary	$30,000
Softie Salary	20,000
Techie Investment (30,000 x 20%)	6,000
Softie Investment (40,000 x 20%)	8,000
Total Allowances	$64,000
Yearly Income	90,000
Excess of Income over Allowances	$26,000

This means that effectively, the partnership has a gain of $26,000 after salaries and investments are allowed for. Each partner will then share equally, or have a $13,000 gain. Example 16.5.3 gives the journal entry for this division of income.

EXAMPLE 16.5.3

The Sample Partnership
General Journal

Date	Acct. No.	Description	Debit	Credit

1992				
Dec 31	40	Revenue and Expense Summary	90,000	
	31	Techie – Capital		49,000
	15	Softie – Capital		41,000

To record the division of 1992 income.

If either of the partners had taken their money out in cash, the credit for their portion would have been to the cash in bank account. The calculations for each partner's share is shown in Table 16.5.4 below.

TABLE 16.5.4

Explanation	Techie	Softie	Total
Salary	$30,000	$20,000	$50,000
Investment	6,000	8,000	14,000
Equal Parts Income	13,000	13,000	26,000
Totals	$49,000	$41,000	$90,000

As can be seen, the sum of the two totals for Techie and Softie is equal to the total income of $90,000.

16.6 PARTNERSHIP STATEMENTS

At the end of an accounting period a statement of the partners' equity can be prepared. This statement would show the beginning balance of each partner's capital account and any withdrawals they may have had for the period. This statement would also show any additional investments for any of the partners.

It would, of course, include any entries for salaries, investments and division of profits and losses. The final number for each partner would be the ending balance in that partner's capital account.

16.7 OTHER CONSIDERATIONS

We have covered the most common accounting problems encountered when working with partnerships. There are a number of other considerations that are beyond the scope of this review. Some of these are the dissolution of a partnership, whether it be because of admission of new partners, death of a partner, or withdrawal of a partner.

A situation where one of more of the partners bring goodwill to the partnership is often encountered. Accounting for this can become very involved, and experts should be contacted.

Last, there is the very real possibility of a liquidation of a partnership. This could be for any of a number of reasons. There could be gains on the liquidation, or losses. It would also be possible to have deficiencies in capital in the case of losses on a liquidation. In this case, the personal assets of the partners would be at risk.

CHAPTER 17

CORPORATIONS

17.1   CORPORATION DEFINED

A corporation is a legal entity with an existence separate and distinct from its owners. A corporation has many of the powers accorded to individuals. A corporation can own property and enter into contracts in its own name. Since it has legal status, a corporation can sue and be sued. Corporations do not possess an individual's right to vote or hold public office.

17.2   ADVANTAGES OF A CORPORATION

Corporations provide several advantages over other forms of business organizations. These are: (1) Stockholders have no personal liability for corporate debts. Creditors have a claim against the assets of a corporation, not those of its owners. The personal risk of each owner is limited to the amount of their investment; (2) Capital can be accumulated easily through the sale of shares of stock in the corporation. These shares represent ownership in the corporation and may be widely held; (3) Ownership interest in the corporation can be easily transferred. Shares of stock of a corporation may be bought and sold without dissolving or disrupting company operations; (4) A corporation is a legal entity with a perpetual existence; (5) Professional management can be hired and supervised by a board of directors elected by stockholders.

17.3   DISADVANTAGES OF A CORPORATION

Disadvantages of a corporate organization are: (1) Corporate income is subject to "double taxation." Operating income of a corporation is subject to Federal (and sometimes state and municipal) income taxes. Income after taxes is then distributed to stockholders through dividends, which are then taxed again as income to individual stockholders; (2) Corporations are subject to a greater degree of State and Federal regulation than other forms of business organization; (3) The separation of ownership and control may contribute to a situation where management may not act in the stockholders' best interests.

17.4   PAR VALUE STOCK

A corporation's articles of incorporation will provide for **authorization** for a specific number of shares of stock and the par value (if any) of that stock. Shares of stock that have been issued are said to be **outstanding**. The number of shares of stock outstanding must be less than or equal to the number of shares authorized. The **par value** represents the legal capital per share. Stockholders' equity cannot be reduced below this amount except by losses from business operations or legal action taken by a majority vote of shareholders. Dividends that would reduce stockholders' equity below the par value of outstanding shares are prohibited in many states.

When par value stock is **issued**, the capital stock account is credited with the par value of the stock issued, regardless of whether the issue price is above or below par. For example, assume that a corporation issues 50,000 shares of $10 par value stock at a price of $20 per share. Example 17.4.1 shows the journal entry necessary to record this transaction.

EXAMPLE 17.4.1

The Sample Company
General Journal

Date	Description	Debit	Credit
	Cash	1,000,000	
	Capital stock		500,000
	Paid-in capital in excess		
	of par		500,000

Paid-in capital represents the excess of the issue price over the par value of the stock.

17.5   NO-PAR STOCK

In some instances, stock may be issued without a par value. In such cases, it is customary for the corporation to indicate a **stated value**, which for accounting purposes serves the same purpose as par value. Using the previous example, assume it is no-par stock with a stated value of $5 per share. Example 17.5.1 shows the entry necessary to record this transaction.

EXAMPLE 17.5.1

The Sample Company
General Journal

Date	Description	Debit	Credit
	Cash	1,000,000	
	Capital stock		250,000
	Paid-in Capital in Excess		
	of Stated Value		750,000

Without a stated value, the entire $1,000,000 would be considered capital stock and subject to the limitations on withdrawal described previously.

17.6 COMMON STOCK

There are two general classes of stocks: common stock and preferred stock. **Common stock** is the most basic form of capital stock. Common stockholders have several basic rights. These include: (1) Common stockholders have the right to be represented in the management of a corporation through election of a board of directors. Approval of major actions, such as a merger or acquisition, selection of independent auditors, or establishment of a stock option plan, may require a majority vote of stockholders. Stockholders receive one vote for each share of stock held in their name, although this vote may be transferred to another through proxy; (2) Stockholders have the right to share in the profits of a corporation by receiving dividends declared by the board of directors; (3) Stockholders have the right to share in the distribution of assets if the corporation is liquidated. Creditors have first claim on corporate assets in such a situation, followed by preferred shareholders, but any remaining assets are divided between common stockholders based on percentage of shares owned; (4) Stockholders have the right of first refusal if a corporation decides to increase the number of shares of stock outstanding. This allows stockholders to maintain their ownership percentage in the company In practice, this right is often waived to provide management with flexibility in issuing new stock.

17.7 PREFERRED STOCK

Another class of capital stock is **preferred stock**. Here the basic rights of common stockholders are modified to some extent. The characteristics of preferred stock include: (1) Preferred stock usually provides for a stated dividend rate that must be paid before any dividends are distributed to common stockholders; (2) In the event of liquidation of the corporation, the claims of preferred stockholders have preference over those of common stockholders. These claims are, however, secondary to those of the corporation's creditors; (3) Preferred stock is usually callable at the option of the corporation; (4) Preferred stockholders have no voting power at stockholders' meetings.

17.8 CONVERTIBLE PREFERRED STOCK

A corporation may offer a conversion privilege which allows owners of preferred stock to convert their shares for common stock according to a specified formula. As an example, assume that a corporation's preferred stock is convertible in a ratio of three $10 par common shares for each share of $50 par preferred stock. Example 17.8.1 shows the entry needed to record conversion of 1,000 preferred shares to common stock.

EXAMPLE 17.8.1

Date	Description	Debit	Credit
	Convertible Preferred Stock	50,000	
	Common Stock		30,000
	Paid-in Capital in Excess of Par Value		20,000

In this example, 1,000 shares of $50 par value preferred stock were converted into 3,000 shares of $10 par value common stock. The $20,000 difference is paid-in capital in excess of par value.

17.9 TREASURY STOCK

When a company purchases its own stock, that stock is said to be placed in the treasury of the company as **treasury stock**. Treasury shares are not retired, but can be held indefinitely and reissued at any time. Shares held as treasury stock are not entitled to vote, receive dividends, or share in assets upon dissolution of the company. Treasury shares are not considered outstanding shares of stock for computation of earnings per share. Example 17.9.1 illustrates the purchase of 1,000 shares of Sample Company common stock by that company for $5,000.

EXAMPLE 17.9.1

Date	Description	Debit	Credit
	Treasury Stock	5,000	
	Cash		5,000

To record the purchase of 1,000 shares of Sample Company stock at $5 per share.

Example 17.9.2 illustrates the entry needed for reissuance of the stock at $6 per share.

EXAMPLE 17.9.2

Date	Description	Debit	Credit
	Cash	6,000	
	Treasury Stock		5,000
	Paid-In-Capital from Treasury Stock Sales		1,000

To record the reissuance of 1,000 shares of treasury stock, with cost of $5 per share, at $6 per share.

No gain or loss is recognized on treasury stock transactions. Treasury stock is shown on the balance sheet as a **deduction** from capital. The common stock account is unaffected by treasury stock transactions.

CHAPTER 18

CORPORATIONS: EARNINGS AND DIVIDENDS

18.1   EQUITY SECTION STRUCTURES

Although there is not an absolute correct structure for the order of accounts listed in the balance sheet equity section, there are a few guidelines that most preparers of financial statements follow. There is also a fair amount of diversity of terms that really mean the same thing. We will look at a few of these items in this chapter as well as consider dividends and **earnings per share** (EPS).

The major section in a balance sheet dealing with the investment of the owners is likely to be titled many different ways. Some of the more common are **Stockholders' Equity, Owners' Equity,** and **Shareholders' Equity**. In all three of those titles, the word "equity" might very well be substituted with "investment." All six terms usually refer to the same thing.

Normally the various classes of stock (Common, Preferred, etc.) and the amounts of each are listed first. Then all additional premiums or discounts on stock transactions are listed. These are then followed by the remaining paid-in capital accounts, which are often lumped into one title on the balance sheet.

18.2 CORPORATE INCOME TAXES

Corporations differ from sole proprietorships and partnerships in that they are a separate legal entity. As such they are subject to income taxes of the federal government as well as states and municipalities. The usual procedure for paying taxes is to pay a quarterly estimate which should be equal to one fourth of the estimated total for the year.

Assume, for instance, that Sample Company estimated their taxes for the year to be $200,000. The entry for each of the first three quarters would be as in Example 18.2.1.

EXAMPLE 18.2.1

The Sample Partnership
General Journal

Date	Acct. No.	Description	Debit	Credit
1992 Mar31	39 1	Income Tax Cash	50,000	50,000

To record first quarter Federal Income Tax.

At the end of the year, any adjustment needed to bring the income tax to the correct total would have to be made. Assume for example that in the example above, that at the end of the year, Sample Company discovered upon doing their tax returns that they really only owned $185,000. The adjusting entry would be as in Example 18.2.2.

EXAMPLE 18.2.2

The Sample Partnership
General Journal

Date	Acct. No.	Description	Debit	Credit
1992 Dec31	2	Accounts Receivable: Income Tax	15,000	
	39	Income Tax		15,000

To record adjustment to 1992 Income Taxes.

If instead of less taxes, the company had more than the amount paid in the four quarters, the entry would have included an additional debit to Income Tax, and a credit to a liability called **Income Tax Payable**.

When working with income taxes, there are two times when the income tax paid will differ from what normally would be determined from the accounts. The first of these is **permanent differences**. In this case, the tax law provides for special consideration of classes of expenses or revenues. These differences are no problem for financial accounting as the amount reported on the financial statements will be the amount determined using the tax laws.

A more involved process evolves when the difference is a **timing difference**. In this case, the amount reported on the financial statements will be different than the amount paid to the taxing authority during the period. Usually the amount paid is less than the amount reported on the financial statements. This difference will usually be reversed in later years.

There are usually one of two reasons that such differences develop. In many cases, GAAP allows for one method of accounting to be used for tax purposes and another for financial statement purposes. This is the most likely reason for a timing difference. The other would be when the company uses an accounting technique that is not generally accepted. In that case the procedure would normally not be acceptable for calculating income tax liability.

18.3 DEFERRED INCOME TAXES

When timing differences occur, there will be a deferral of income taxes to a later period. This will usually entail setting up an account called **Deferred Income Taxes Payable** and crediting it for the difference between current taxes to be paid and the amount shown on the financial statements as income tax expense. In later periods, the deferral should be reduced.

To illustrate, let us assume that all the information in Table 18.3 was provided on Sample Company.

TABLE 18.3

SAMPLE COMPANY
Selected Data

Taxable income per company financial records	$500,000	
Income tax calculated on $500,000 at 40%		$200,000
Taxable income per company tax return	$300,000	
Income tax based on $300,000 at 40%		$120,000
Income tax to be deferred to later years		$ 80,000

Example 18.3.1 gives the journal entry to formally recognize this timing difference.

EXAMPLE 18.3.1

The Sample Company
General Journal

Date	Acct. No.	Description	Debit	Credit
1992 Dec31	39	Income Tax	200,000	
	65	Income Tax Payable		120,000
	43	Deferred Income Tax Payable		80,000

To recognize income tax expense for 1992 and set up deferral.

The income tax payable will be a current liability. The deferred income tax payable may be in two groupings. That amount that will be due in one year will be a current liability. The rest will go after long-term liabilities on the balance sheet. In later years the reverse situation should come about. At that point an entry will need to be made to reduce the deferred income tax account. Assume that in 1994, $40,000 of the deferred Income Tax Payable was to be paid. The entry for this reduction is shown in Example 18.3.2.

EXAMPLE 18.3.2

The Sample Company
General Journal

Date	Acct. No.	Description	Debit	Credit
1994 Dec31	43	Deferred Income Tax Payable	40,000	
	65	Income Tax Payable		40,000

To reclassify Deferred Taxes Payable to a current account.

18.4   UNUSUAL ITEMS

In attempting to give as much information as possible in the financial statements of a company, accountants have developed four categories of unusual items that require special reporting.

The first of these is **prior period adjustments.** These are changes made in net income from earlier periods. These will appear as adjustments to the beginning retained earnings balance of the period the adjustment is made. This will be done on the retained earnings statement. The adjustment will be stated net of related income tax effect. The tax effect should be stated in the adjustment.

Discontinued operations is the second category that deserves special attention. When an organization sells, closes, or in some other way disposes of a segment of the business, a gain or loss will normally result. To be sure these are not mixed in with operations that will be ongoing, this item will be shown as a **gain or loss from discontinued operations** net of related taxes. This will be done on the income statement. Footnotes to the financial statements should disclose the details of the segment that was discontinued.

Gains or losses that occur as a result of transactions that are both unusual in nature and happen infrequently are termed **extraordinary items**. As a result of the strict guidelines established, very few items meet both criteria. Those that do, will be shown on the income statement, net of related tax effect.

It is not unusual for a company to adopt a generally accepted accounting principle different from one it had been using. This will likely cause an effect of prior period income figures as well as for the current period. This adjustment will be called **change in accounting principle**, and be shown on the income statement in two parts. The cumulative effect of the change on prior periods net income will be shown as a special item. The second step will be to show the effect on net income for the current period.

18.5 EARNINGS PER SHARE

As a result of difference in size of companies, it is difficult to compare multiple companies in a specific industry or region. One way to assist in this comparison is to calculate the **earnings per share of common stock** (EPS). This is the number that is most often reported in the financial press and in the news. By reducing the earnings to a number per share of common stock, comparisons are easier to make.

If there is just common stock outstanding, the EPS can be arrived at by dividing net income by the number of shares of stock outstanding. If preferred stock also exists, the amount of preferred dividends required would be subtracted from net income before dividing by the number of shares outstanding.

It is normal to show the EPS for all of the categories of unusual items discussed earlier in this chapter as separate items. If other classes of stock exist or bonds exist that could be converted into common stock, the net income would need to be **diluted** to show the effect of these other potential shares. Calculations for fully diluted earnings per share can be extremely complicated and are beyond the scope of this review.

18.6 RETAINED EARNINGS APPROPRIATIONS

When a board of directors of a company wants to limit the amount of dividends that can be paid from retained earnings, they can **appropriate** or **reserve** the amount in a separate classification on the balance sheet. This may be done as a result of a contract, state law, or some other situation that requires the appropriation. The appropriated portion would appear above the unappropriated in the retained earnings section of the balance sheet.

Example 18.6.1 shows the two journal entries required to appropriate retained earnings and to eliminate the appropriation a year later.

EXAMPLE 18.6.1

The Sample Company
General Journal

Date	Acct. No.	Description	Debit	Credit
1992 Dec31	31 32	Retained Earnings Appropriated Retained Earnings–Bonds	200,000	200,000

To appropriate retained earnings for bond redemption.

Date	Acct. No.	Description	Debit	Credit
1993 Dec31	32 31	Appropriated Retained Earnings–Bonds Retained Earnings	200,000	200,000

To eliminate the appropriation for retained earnings for bonds.

An appropriation of retained earnings **does not** mean there is actually that amount of money set aside. If money **is** set aside as cash or securities, the appropriation is said to be **funded.**

Appropriations need not be formalized in the financial statements in the form of journal entries. They can just be noted in footnotes that contain the details of the appropriation.

18.7   CASH DIVIDENDS

Cash dividends are a distribution of corporate earnings to the stockholders in the form of cash. This is the most usual form of dividends. There are three important dates involved with cash dividends. They are:

1.   Date of declaration–this is the date the formal announcement of a cash dividend was made.

2.   Date of record–people owning shares on this date will receive the cash dividend.

3.   Date of payment–this is the day the actual cash dividend is paid.

Cash dividends are usually declared as a percent of par or stated value. If a company had 20,000 shares of stock at a par value of $10, the entry for a 5% cash dividend would be:

$$20,000 \times \$10 \times .05 = \$10,000$$

Example 18.7.1 gives the journal entries for declaration of the dividend and then the payment of the dividend. The date of declaration was November 30, 1992. The date of payment was February 10, 1993.

EXAMPLE 18.7.1

The Sample Company
General Journal

Date	Acct. No.	Description	Debit	Credit
1992 Nov30	93	Cash Dividends	10,000	
	62	Cash Dividends Payable		10,000

To record the declaration of a 5% cash dividend.

1993 Feb10	62	Cash Dividends Payable	10,000	
	1	Cash		10,000

To record payment of cash dividend declared on November 30, 1992.

The cash dividends will be closed to retained earnings at the end of the accounting period.

18.8 STOCK DIVIDENDS

When a corporation is not able (or does not want to) pay cash dividends, they may issue a **stock dividend**. This is usually done when they have losses, or want to retain funds for expansion. Using the information from above, assuming the dividend was a stock dividend rather than cash, the entry will be as in Example 18.8.1. The debit to Stock Dividends will be closed to retained earnings.

EXAMPLE 18.8.1

The Sample Company
General Journal

Date	Acct. No.	Description	Debit	Credit
1992 Nov30	94	Stock Dividends	10,000	
	63	Stock Dividends Distributable		10,000

To record the declaration of a 5% stock dividend.

Date	Acct. No.	Description	Debit	Credit
1993 Feb10	63	Stock Dividends Distributable	10,000	
	38	Common Stock		10,000

To record payment of stock dividend declared on November 30, 1992.

18.9   STOCK SPLITS

Stock splits occur when a company issues a proportionate number of additional shares to the stockholders. This will have the effect of reducing the par or stated value per share. It is usually done to reduce the market price per share to encourage more small investors to buy company shares. This is also called a **stock split.**

The value of each stockholder's investment will remain the same, only the number of shares will change. There is no formal entry in the company's books. However, the new financial statements should reflect the new number of shares outstanding.

18.10 EFFECT OF TREASURY STOCK

If treasury stock exists, cash dividends will not be paid on the treasury stock. In the case of stock dividends, the dividend can be paid on shares outstanding, or shares issued. Both are acceptable. Treasury stock may be included in a stock split.

CHAPTER 19

CONSOLIDATIONS

19.1 PARENT AND SUBSIDIARY COMPANY RELATIONSHIPS

A corporation which owns more than 50% of the common stock of another corporation is known as a **parent company**. A company that is majority owned by another corporation is known as a **subsidiary**. The parent controls election of the subsidiary's board of directors (and therefore all company activities) through exercise of voting rights associated with its majority stock ownership. In effect, parent and subsidiary companies operate as one entity controlled by directors of the parent company.

Since a parent company and its subsidiaries are separate legal entities, separate financial statements are prepared for each company. In the separate financial statements for the parent company, subsidiaries appear only as investments. In recognition of the fact that parent and subsidiaries function as one entity, **consolidated** financial statements are also prepared. In consolidated financial statements, assets, liabilities, revenue, and expenses of two or more separate corporations are combined in a single set of financial statements.

19.2 INTERCOMPANY ELIMINATIONS

To accurately reflect the financial position of a parent and its subsidiaries on a consolidated basis, it is necessary to eliminate the effects of **intercompany transactions**. These transactions may include intercompany loans, property leases, or sales of inventory or equipment. Viewing a parent and its subsidiaries as one entity, those assets or liabilities that are simply transfers from one part of the entity to another should be eliminated.

19.3 PREPARATION OF CONSOLIDATED FINANCIAL STATEMENTS

19.3.1 PURCHASE METHOD

One method of accounting for acquisition of one company by another is the **purchase method**. This method is used when the stock of a subsidiary is acquired by cash payment. It is also used when a parent issues bonds payable or capital stock to acquire the stock of a subsidiary company.

In preparing consolidated financial statements, a worksheet is used to determine the necessary elimination entries. These entries are used for this purpose only. They are not recorded in the financial records of the parent or its subsidiaries. As shown in Example 19.3.1, the worksheet contains the asset and liability account balances for the parent and each subsidiary. Debit and credit columns are provided for intercompany eliminations and a column is provided for the **consolidated** asset and liability account balances. In this example, assume that Smith Corporation purchased 100% of the stock of Jones Corporation for $100,000 cash on January 1, 1999. On that same date, Smith Corporation lends $50,000 to Jones Corporation for working capital purposes. Jones Corporation executes a note payable to Smith Corporation to evidence the loan.

EXAMPLE 19.3.1

SMITH CORPORATION AND SUBSIDIARY
Worksheet for Consolidated Balance Sheet
January 1, 1999 (Date of Acquisition)
(in 000's)

	Smith Corp.	Jones Corp.	Intercompany Eliminations Debit	Intercompany Eliminations Credit	Cons. Bal. Sheet
Cash	60	40			100
Receivables:					
Notes	50			50	
Accounts (net)	45	32			77
Inventories	75	50			125
Investment in Jones					
Corporation	100			100	
Property, Plant and					
Equipment	55	50			105
Total	385	172			407
Notes Payable		50	50		
Accounts Payable	33	22			55
Capital Stock:					
Smith Corporation	200				200
Jones Corporation		40	40		
Retained Earnings:					
Smith Corporation	152				152
Jones Corporation		60	60		
Total	385	172	150	150	407

Intercompany eliminations include elimination of (1) intercompany debt, (2) intercompany stock ownership, and (3) intercompany revenue and expenses. In the above example, the loan from the parent Smith Corporation to its subsidiary (Jones Corporation) is eliminated from the consolidated balance sheet since the effect would be to artificially inflate the consolidated assets and liabilities. The $100,000 purchase price of Jones Corporation (carried as an investment on Smith's books and as capital stock and retained earnings for Jones) is eliminated for the same reason. The consolidated balance sheet for Smith Corporation and its subsidiary can now be prepared from the figures shown in the worksheet.

19.4   PURCHASE PRICE ABOVE BOOK VALUE

There may be occasions when a parent will pay more for the stock of a subsidiary company than is reflected in the stockholders' equity accounts. A parent company may feel that the subsidiary's assets are undervalued or the prospects for future growth or profits may justify a higher purchase price. This excess of purchase price over stockholders' equity is known as **goodwill**. Using the previous example, assume that Smith Corporation pays $150,000 cash for Jones Corporation although the stockholders' equity of Jones Corporation is only $100,000. The eliminations needed in this situation are shown in Example 19.4.1.

Note that again the entire amount of Smith's investment in Jones is eliminated by crediting that account for $150,000. Debits are to goodwill ($50,000), Jones Corporation capital stock ($40,000), and Jones Corporation retained earnings ($60,000).

EXAMPLE 19.4.1

SMITH CORPORATION AND SUBSIDIARY
Worksheet for Consolidated Balance Sheet
January 1, 1999 (Date of Acquisition)
(In 000's)

	Smith Corp.	Jones Corp.	Intercompany Eliminations Debit	Intercompany Eliminations Credit	Cons. Bal. Sheet
Cash	60	40			100
Receivables:					
Notes	50			50	
Accounts (net)	45	32			77
Inventories	75	50			125
Investment in Jones					
Corporation	150			150	
Goodwill			50		50
Property, Plant and					
Equipment	55	50			105
Total	435	172			457
Notes Payable		50	50		
Accounts Payable	33	22			55
Capital Stock:					
Smith Corporation	200				200
Jones Corporation		40	40		
Retained Earnings:					
Smith Corporation	202				202
Jones Corporation		60	60		
Total	435	172	200	200	457

137

EXAMPLE 19.5.1

SMITH CORPORATION AND SUBSIDIARY
Worksheet for Consolidated Balance Sheet
January 1, 1999 (Date of Acquisition)
(In 000's)

	Smith Corp.	Jones Corp.	Intercompany Eliminations Debit	Intercompany Eliminations Credit	Cons. Bal. Sheet
Cash	60	40			100
Receivables:					
Notes	50			50	
Accounts (net)	45	32			77
Inventories	75	50			125
Investment in Jones					
Corporation	75			75	
Property, Plant and					
Equipment	55	50			105
Total	360	172			407
Notes Payable		50	50		
Accounts Payable	33	22			55
Capital Stock:					
Smith Corporation	200				200
Jones Corporation		40	30(1) 10(2)		
Retained Earnings:					
Smith Corporation	127				127
Jones Corporation		60	45(1) 15(2)		
Minority Interest				25	25
Total	360	172	150	150	407

(1) To eliminate Smith Corporation's 75% interest.
(2) To classify remaining 25% as minority interest.

138

19.5 PURCHASE OF LESS THAN 100% OF SUBSIDIARY

If a parent company purchases less than 100% (but still a majority) of the stock of a subsidiary, a **minority interest** will appear on the consolidated balance sheet. This minority interest represents the stock held by stockholders other than the parent company. In this situation, only the portion of the subsidiary's stockholder's equity owned by the parent is eliminated. Again using the previous example, assume that Smith Corporation purchases 75% of Jones Corporation for $75,000. Stockholders' equity for Jones Corporation is $100,000. The eliminations necessary are shown in Example 19.5.1.

19.6 CONSOLIDATED INCOME STATEMENT

A consolidated income statement, like the consolidated balance sheet, is prepared by combining revenue and expense accounts for the parent and subsidiary companies. Items to be eliminated during consolidation of income statements include: (1) Intercompany sales; (2) Cost of goods sold resulting from intercompany sales; (3) Interest expense on intercompany loans; (4) Interest revenue from intercompany loans; (5) Rent or income received for services to affiliated companies; (6) Rent or expenses paid for services from affiliated companies.

19.7 POOLING OF INTEREST METHOD

If the stock of a subsidiary is acquire in exchange for shares of the parent company's stock and if certain other criteria are met, a business combination may be treated as a **pooling of interest**. In this situation, stockholders of the subsidiary become stockholders of the parent company. The stockholders of the two companies are said to have pooled their interests, rather than one party selling out to the other. Since there is no real purchase or sale, the assets of the subsidiary are not revalued and no goodwill is recorded. Another difference between this method and the purchase method is that under the pooling of interests method, earnings of the subsidiary for the entire year in which the affiliation occurs are included in the consolidated income statement. Under the purchase method, earnings of the subsidiary are combined with those of the parent only from the date of acquisition.

CHAPTER 20

STATEMENT OF CASH FLOWS

20.1 PURPOSE OF STATEMENT OF CASH FLOWS

According to the Financial Accounting Standards Board, the purpose of the **statement of cash flows** is to provide information about cash receipts and payments as well as information about the operating, investing and financing activities of a business.

The statement of cash flows should aid users to: (1) Assess the probability of positive future cash flows; (2) Assess the ability to meet financial obligations; (3) Assess reasons for difference between income and cash flow; (4) Assess cash and non-cash aspects of financing transactions.

The statement of cash flows is composed of three major sections. **Cash flows from operating activities** consist of the cash effects of transactions that determine income. **Cash flows from investing activities** include lending activities, securities transactions, and acquisition and sale of productive assets. **Cash flows from financing activities** include transactions related to obtaining resources from owners and creditors.

20.2 PREPARATION OF THE STATEMENT OF CASH FLOWS

20.2.1 THE WORKSHEET APPROACH

There are several approaches to the preparation of the statement of cash flows; however, for simplicity, the following example concerns only one – the worksheet approach. Using this approach, a four column spreadsheet is prepared with account balances at the beginning of the period in column one and account balances at period end in column four. Columns two and three will be used for debit and credit analysis, respectively.

Example 20.2.1 shows a worksheet prepared for Smith Corporation for the year ended December 31, 1999. Note that accounts with debit balances are listed first, followed by accounts with credit balances.

The debit and credit analysis is simple. For debit accounts that show an increased balance at year-end, the amount of the increase is entered in the debit column (column two). Net decreases in asset balances are entered in the credit column (column three). For credit accounts that show an increased balance at year-end, the amount of increase is entered in the credit column. Decreases are entered in the debit column (column two). The totals of debit and credit balances should be equal.

20.2.2 COMPLETION OF THE STATEMENT OF CASH FLOWS

Using the transaction information from the worksheet, it is relatively simple to complete the statement of cash flows. As shown in Example 20.2.2, the statement contains the three major sections (cash flows from operating activities, investing activities, and financing activities), with detailed account transactions from the worksheet. The net change in cash shown in the statement of cash flows should be equal to the amount of change in cash shown in the worksheet.

EXAMPLE 20.2.1

SMITH CORPORATION
Worksheet for Statement of Cash Flows
For the Year Ended December 31, 1999

Summary of 1999 Entries

	Jan. 1 Balance	Debit	Credit	Dec. 31 Balance
Debits				
Cash	25,000		5,000	20,000
Accounts Receivable	40,000	10,000		50,000
Inventory	65,000	20,000		85,000
Prepaid Expenses	7,500		1,000	6,500
Land	50,000			50,000
Buildings	75,000	15,000		90,000
Equipment	35,000	20,000		55,000
Patents	9,000		2,000	7,000
Total Debits	306,500	65,000	8,000	363,500
Credits				
Accumulated Deprecation	25,000		17,000	42,000
Accounts Payable	35,000	4,000		31,000
Accrued Liabilities	28,000		8,000	36,000
Bonds Payable	100,000			100,000
Premium on Bonds Payable	6,000	500		5,500
Common Stock	20,000		20,000	40,000
Retained Earnings	92,500		16,500	109,000
Total Credits	306,500	4,500	61,500	363,500
Summary Entry Totals		69,500	69,500	

EXAMPLE 20.2.2

SMITH CORPORATION
Statement of Cash Flows
For the Year Ended December 31, 1999

Net Cash from Operating Activities:

Net Income		16,500
Noncash Expenses, Revenues, Losses, and Gains Included in Income:		
Increases:		
Decrease in Prepaid Expenses	1,000	
Increase in Accrued Liabilities	8,000	
Depreciation Expense	17,000	
Patent Amortization	2,000	28,000
Decreases:		
Increase in Accounts Receivable	10,000	
Increase in Inventory	20,000	
Decrease in Accounts Payable	4,000	
Amortization of Bond Premium	500	34,500
Net Cash Flow from Operating Activities		(6,500)
Cash Flows from Investing Activities:		
Decreases:		
Cash used in purchase equipment	20,000	
Cash used to purchase buildings	15,000	(35,000)
Cash Flows form Financing Activities:		
Increases:		
Cash from sale of common stock		20,000
Net Decrease in Cash		(5,000)

CHAPTER 21

FINANCIAL STATEMENT ANALYSIS

21.1 COMPARATIVE FINANCIAL STATEMENTS

Comparative financial statement analysis involves examination of financial statements for a single company for 2 or more accounting periods (years, quarters, or months) and noting the change in both amount and percentage between periods. This form of analysis provides evidence of significant changes in individual accounts and can give a user valuable insight into items that should be further investigated.

21.2 TREND ANALYSIS

Trend analysis is a form of comparative analysis, but instead of examining the entire balance sheet and income statement for two years, this form of analysis involves examination of selected financial statement information over longer periods of time (usually at least 5 years and as much as 10 - 20 years). Trend analysis is performed by selecting a **base year**, for example 1980, and assigning a value of 100% to the amount of the selected financial statement item or items. Each successive year would be compared to the base year on a percentage basis. To illustrate, sales, cost of goods sold, and net income for years 1980 through 1986 and the resulting trend percentages are shown in Example 21.2.1.

EXAMPLE 21.2.1

(in millions)	1980	1981	1982	1983	1984	1985	1986
Sales	10.0	15.0	19.0	25.0	31.0	40.0	50.0
Gross Profit	5.0	8.5	10.0	14.0	18.0	24.0	30.0
Net Income	3.5	4.5	6.5	8.0	10.0	12.5	15.0

% Analysis Based on 1980 Base Year

	1980	1981	1982	1983	1984	1985	1986
Sales	100%	150%	190%	250%	310%	400%	500%
Gross Profit	100	170	200	280	360	480	600
Net Income	100	129	186	229	286	357	428

Using this example, the benefits of trend analysis become evident. Analysis of the actual sales, gross profit, and income data indicates continuing growth in sales and income. Trend analysis, however, shows a different picture. Income is continuing to increase, but at a slower percentage than sales. This, combined with the indication that gross profit is increasing faster than sales, may indicate that management is doing a good job of continuing to reduce material and direct labor costs, but is not controlling administrative or overhead expenses. This indicates a need for further investigation as to the cause of this trend.

21.3.1 COMMON-SIZE FINANCIAL STATEMENTS

Relating financial statement items to each other within a single time period is known as **vertical analysis**. Common-size financial statements show each financial statement item as a percentage of a key item in that statement. For example, a common-size income statement might present each income and

146

expense item as a percentage of sales for that period. Example 21.3.1 shows a common-size income statement for Jade Corporation.

EXAMPLE 21.3.1

JADE CORPORATION
Common-Size Income Statement
For the Year Ended 1999

Sales	100.0%
Cost of Goods Sold	(55.5)
Gross Profit	44.5
Operating Expenses:	
Selling	(18.9)
General and Administrative	(12.5)
Total Operating Expenses	(31.4)
Income Before Income Tax	13.1
Income Tax Expense	(6.0)
Net Income	7.1%

This form of analysis may be used in combination with horizontal analysis method such as comparative statements to detect significant changes in financial statement components form year to year. Common-size statements are particularly useful in comparing companies of different size.

21.3.2 FINANCIAL RATIOS

Another form of vertical analysis is the use of financial ratios. There are many ratios used by financial analysts, but thirteen of the more common ratios used are outlined in Table 21.3.1.

TABLE 21.3.1

FINANCIAL RATIOS

Ratios to Gauge Earnings Performance

Rate of return on total assets =

$$\frac{\text{income before interest expense}}{\text{average total assets}}$$

Rate of return on common stockholders' equity =

$$\frac{\text{net income} - \text{preferred dividends}}{\text{average common stockholders' equity}}$$

Earnings per share =

$$\frac{\text{net income} - \text{preferred dividends}}{\text{average number of common shares outstanding}}$$

Price-earnings ratio =

$$\frac{\text{net income} - \text{preferred dividends}}{\text{earnings per share of common stock}}$$

Dividend yield rate=

$$\frac{\text{dividends per share of common stock}}{\text{current market price per share of common stock}}$$

Ratios to Gauge Debt-Paying Ability

Times interest earned =

$$\frac{\text{income before interest expense and income taxes}}{\text{annual interest expense}}$$

Debt to total assets =

$$\frac{\text{total liabilities}}{\text{total assets}}$$

Stockholders' equity to total assets =

$$\frac{\text{total stockholders' equity}}{\text{total assets}}$$

Financial Ratios to Gauge Liquidity

Current ratio =

$$\frac{\text{current assets}}{\text{current liabilities}}$$

Quick ratio =

$$\frac{\text{quick assets}}{\text{current liabilities}}$$

Inventory turnover =

$$\frac{\text{cost of goods sold}}{\text{average merchandise inventory}}$$

Accounts receivable turnover =

$$\frac{\text{credit sales}}{\text{average accounts receivable}}$$

Average age of receivables =

$$\frac{\text{365 days}}{\text{accounts receivable turnover}}$$

Ratios are most useful when compared to a standard. These standards can be obtained by analyzing financial statements of companies in the same industry or through the use of industry averages provided by trade associations and research firms. Ratios are more meaningful when the companies studies are in the same industry, approximately the same size, and use similar accounting methods.

21.4   OTHER SOURCES OF FINANCIAL INFORMATION

Thorough analysis of financial statements should include a review of the **auditor's report,** where the auditor expresses an opinion as to whether the financial information being presented conforms to generally accepted accounting principles. Any significant deviation from such principles will be noted.

Another source of information are the notes to the financial statements, which outline the various accounting methods used in those statements. Also contained in the financial statement notes is information as to **contingent liabilities** facing the company. These are liabilities that the company may suffer under certain circumstances. The notes should contain information about such contingencies, including the probability of loss to the company involved. Contingencies that are probable in nature and can be reasonably estimated must be shown on the balance sheet as a liability. Other descriptive notes may include information on pension plans, income taxes, and long-term debts.

CHAPTER 22

A COST SYSTEM FOR A JOBBING PLANT

A COST-ACCOUNTING SYSTEM should provide cost figures that will enable management to make decisions such as the following for each type of goods manufactured:

> How profitable is the product at present prices?
> Can it be profitably produced to sell at a different price?
> At what price shall it be sold?
> Should its production level be expanded (or reduced)?
> What can be done to control costs that are out of line?

If only a few kinds of products are made and the manufacturing processes are always the same, these decisions can be made on the basis of average per-unit cost figures computed each month. Either of two methods can be used to compute the average costs: (1) Divide the total manufacturing cost by the number of product units produced. (2) Compute the unit costs of the individual processes and total them. In both cases, in figuring the number of units produced, changes in the inventory in process must be taken into consideration.

Suppose, on the other hand, that many different types of products are made and that selling-price agreements are based on recorded costs. This is likely to be the case where a jobbing plant produces goods for many different customers to the individual customer's specifications, or for a single customer whose specifications change often.

In such cases, the cost-accounting system must be set up so that product costs can be determined more directly. These systems are referred to as *job cost systems* or *production-order cost systems*. If each product unit requires a large dollar outlay, costs are assigned directly to each unit. For less costly units, costs may be assigned to groups or batches of like items and unit costs computed as an average for each group.

Journals and Ledgers

The cost accounting system for any manufacturing enterprise should include an integrated group of journals, ledgers, basic cost records, and control records. The number and kinds of journals and ledgers will depend on (1) the type and volume of transactions with outsiders and (2) the type and volume of cost transfers made necessary by the manufacturing techniques.

For a very small shop, a combined journal from which all postings to general and factory ledger accounts can be made is satisfactory. If the volume of entries is large enough to require several persons for the bookkeeping, separate books of original entry such as the following will be needed:

1. Voucher register
2. Check register
3. Cash receipts journal
4. Sales journal
5. Factory journal
6. Payroll journal

If all activities—manufacturing, administrative, and selling—are carried on in a single location, a general ledger with some subsidiary records is adequate. Subsidiary records will be needed for production jobs and certain other items such as accounts receivable, raw materials, and accounts payable.

If the general office is not at the same location as the factory, it is usually best to use a factory ledger in addition to the general ledger. Reciprocal accounts in each of the ledgers show the net balances of the accounts in the other ledger and so provide for self-balancing. In this way, many of the details of accounting for manufacturing costs can be confined to the factory ledger.

Control and Cost Procedures for a Job-Order Plant

The distinctive features of a job-order cost system are primarily in the basic cost and control records. The following is a typical set of these records:

Orders and reports containing physical-product information:
    Production order
    Production control record
    Daily production report
    Route card, or job-order instruction card

Orders and reports containing both physical-product and dollar-cost information:
    Material requisition
    Job timecard
    Job-cost record
    Production-cost summary

Control Records

The orders and reports containing physical-product information only—such as production orders or daily production reports—are control records. They are used primarily in the plant work areas for scheduling and planning production.

PRODUCTION ORDERS. Exhibit 1 shows a typical production order form. This form is used by the production manager to initiate production activity. When a job is ready for production, or when the inventory of finished products needs building up, the production manager authorizes the start of work by issuing a production order. He keeps one copy and sends a copy with the necessary instructions to each department or machine operator to be involved in the production.

This procedure provides a means for establishing production priorities and makes it possible for all departments or operators to plan for jobs that are coming up. Each department or operator keeps a file of pending orders arranged by the expected sequence of work. The foreman or the production manager can then check from time to time and readjust the job sequence as needed. The aim, of course, is to make sure that successive operations on all orders are scheduled as efficiently as possible.

When manufacturing operations are highly mechanized and the volume of production near capacity, machine loading is of prime importance. In such cases, an employee or group of employees may be assigned to analyze production orders and

Exhibit 1.—Production order

PRODUCTION ORDER

ORDER NO. _____ DATE ISSUED _____

FOR _____ OR STOCK _____
PURCHASER

SCHEDULED COMPLETION DATE _____

PRODUCT DESCRIPTION _____

NO. OF ITEMS _____ DRAWING NO. _____ PATTERN NO. _____

MATERIAL REQUISITION NOS. _____

INSTRUCTIONS:

DATE COMPLETED _____

NO. OF GOOD UNITS _____

NO. OF DEFECTIVE UNITS _____
FOREMAN OR SUPERVISOR

schedule the machines so as to get the maximum use from the plant's facilities.

PRODUCTION CONTROL RECORD. The person responsible for control of production needs some sort of record or file to show the status of all jobs in process. A typical production control record is shown as exhibit 2.

Exhibit 2.—Production control record

PRODUCTION CONTROL RECORD									
ORDER NO.	DATE ISSUED	- PRODUCT DESCRIPTION	NO. OF ITEMS	SCHEDULED COMPLETION	PURCHASER OR FOR STOCK	DEPARTMENTS OR OPERATIONS	DATE COMPL.	NO. OF GOOD ITEMS	REMARKS

When the production manager issues a production order, he enters the order number and other details on the production control record. In the column headed "Departments or operations," the numbers or other identifying codes of all departments that will work on the job are entered. As the order moves through the factory, one department after another is checked off, showing where the job stands at any time.

The production control record is thus an up-to-date running history of all production activity. It shows where the factory stands in terms of jobs, units of product, and stages of completion. It is a means of control over all work in process. Furthermore, it is a ready source of information when customers ask about their orders. The information should also be

156

used, along with sales orders or forecasts and stock records of finished products, to determine the need for new production orders.

The form shown as exhibit 2 is just an example. How elaborate a form is needed depends on a number of factors— the number of operations, the number of jobs usually in process at one time, the length of time required to finish each job, the amount of detailed information needed by management. If production operations are numerous or jobs differ greatly, it may be better to use separate control cards (filed numerically) for each job. The production order form (exhibit 1) can be used for this.

Other methods can be used to control production—blackboard and chalk, pegboard layouts, mechanical visual aids, electronic

Exhibit 3.—Daily production report

DAILY PRODUCTION REPORT FOR _____ DATE					
ORDER NO	PRODUCT DESCRIPTION	DEPT.	NO. OF ITEMS FINISHED	NO. OF ITEMS SPOILED, LOST, OR WASTED	REMARKS

equipment. The best method for a small manufacturing firm is the one it finds easy to understand and whose cost in money and time it can afford.

DAILY PRODUCTION REPORT. The daily production report (exhibit 3) provides the data for recording job progress on the production control record. Each morning the production manager should see that the preceding day's production is checked for each department or operation and recorded on the daily production report.

If each job calls for only one product unit, or very few units, the entries should show only the *jobs* completed by each department. If each job is made up of a large number of product units and requires at least several days to complete, a more

Exhibit 4.—Route card or job order instruction card

ROUTE CARD			
PRODUCTION ORDER NO. _____			
PRODUCT _____			
NO. OF UNITS _____			
SPECIAL INSTRUCTIONS:			
REQUIRED OPERATIONS	DEPT.	DATE COMPL.	INITIALS OF FOREMAN OR OPERATOR

detailed record is needed. For such jobs, it is important to show the number of individual units completed by each department so that the stage of completion of each job in each department may be known.

Showing on the daily report the number of units lost, wasted, or spoiled uncovers trouble spots promptly. If necessary, future operations on the jobs in process can be rescheduled.

ROUTE CARD OR JOB-ORDER INSTRUCTION CARD. Route cards help direct the movement of jobs through the plant. They also

158

Exhibit 5.—Cost records and accounts for a job-order plant

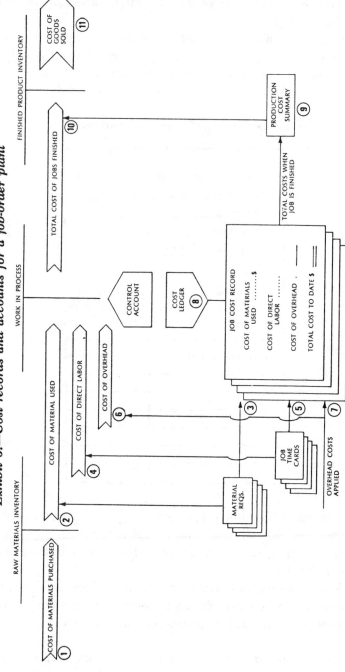

For an explanation of the circled numbers in this diagram, refer to the section of this chapter titled "Recording Job Costs"

serve as a running history that can be used to trace responsibility for either substandard workmanship or exceptional efficiency.

A route card, or job-order instruction card (exhibit 4), should be prepared before each production order is issued. This card goes to the department or employee who will work on the order first and then accompanies the job through all operations. Each employee or foreman handling the job enters on the card the date the employee's operation is completed and his or her initials.

Recording Job Costs

The techniques discussed so far are control techniques. The forms shown in exhibits 1 through 4 are in terms of units rather than dollars and cents. They tell what, how much, and where, but not how much money is involved in the units and activity. Other records are needed to gather product cost information.

For a jobbing plant, the four basic cost records, already listed on pg. 154, are the materials requisition, the job time card, the job cost record, and the production cost summary. These basic cost records should tie in with the overall accounting system. Their relation to accounts in the general or factory ledger is shown in exhibit 5. (The section numbers in the explanation that follows refer to the corresponding circled numbers in exhibit 5.)

1. The *cost of materials purchased* is recorded in the Raw Materials Inventory account from vendors' invoices. The entry will read as follows:

	Debit	Credit
Raw materials inventory	xxx	
Accounts payable		xxx

To record the purchase of raw materials.

2. The *Materials Requisition* (exhibit 6) is used to authorize all withdrawals from a storeroom or stock of raw materials. The requisitions should be prepared by someone who knows exactly what materials are needed for the job—for example, the plan-

Exhibit 6.—Material requisition

```
┌─────────────────────────────────────────────────────────────────┐
│                    MATERIAL REQUISITION                           │
│   DATE_____    REQUISITION  NO. _____   │
│                                                                   │
│   FOR _____      PRODUCTION ORDER NO. _____  │
│            DEPARTMENT OR OPERATOR                                 │
│   REQUESTED BY_____         │
├───────┬──────────┬───────────────┬────────┬──────┬────────────────┤
│STORES │ QUANTITY │               │ QUAN.  │ UNIT │                │
│ NO.   │REQUESTED │ DESCRIPTION    │ISSUED  │ COST │  TOTAL COST    │
├───────┼──────────┼───────────────┼────────┼──────┼────────────────┤
│       │          │               │        │      │                │
├───────┼──────────┼───────────────┼────────┼──────┼────────────────┤
│       │          │               │        │      │                │
├───────┼──────────┼───────────────┼────────┼──────┼────────────────┤
│       │          │               │        │      │                │
├───────┼──────────┼───────────────┼────────┼──────┼────────────────┤
│       │          │               │        │      │                │
├───────┼──────────┼───────────────┼────────┼──────┼────────────────┤
│       │          │               │        │      │                │
├───────┼──────────┼───────────────┼────────┼──────┼────────────────┤
│       │          │               │        │      │                │
├───────┼──────────┼───────────────┼────────┼──────┼────────────────┤
│       │          │               │        │      │                │
├───────┴──────────┴───────────────┴────────┴──────┴────────────────┤
│                                                                   │
│   RECEIVED BY_____  DATE _____           │
└─────────────────────────────────────────────────────────────────┘
```

ning department, production engineer, or production manager. Only authorized individuals should sign requisitions.

If more materials must be issued to a job already started, it may mean too much waste or spoilage. A colored requisition for added-on issues will call attention to this possibility.

The materials costs entered on the requisition are based on the unit costs shown in the Raw Materials Inventory account. They are the basic record from which a journal entry is made to transfer costs from the Raw Materials Inventory to the Work-in-Process account, as follows:

	Debit	Credit
Work in process	xxx	
Raw materials inventory		xxx

To transfer materials cost to work-in-process account.

3. The materials requisition is also the basic cost record for recording materials costs on the *Job Cost Record* (exhibits 7 and 8). Direct labor and overhead costs will be added to give the total manufacturing costs of each job.

Exhibit 7.—Job-cost record for a departmentalized plant

JOB COST RECORD

FOR _____   ORDER NO. _____

PRODUCT_____   QUANTITY _____

DATE WANTED_____ DATE STARTED_____ DATE COMPLETED_____

DIRECT MATERIALS

DATE	DEPT.	REQ. NO.	STORES NO.	QUANTITY	COST PER UNIT	TOTAL COST

DIRECT LABOR

DATE	DEPT.	TIME CARD NO.	DESCRIPTION	HRS. OR PCS.	RATE	TOTAL COST

APPLIED OVERHEAD

DATE	DEPT.	BASIS	RATE	TOTAL COST

SUMMARY FOR ORDER NO. _____

DIRECT MATERIALS _____
DIRECT LABOR   _____
APPLIED OVERHEAD _____

TOTAL FACTORY COST   _____
FACTORY COST PER UNIT   _____

4. Before each production order is run, the planning department or the department foreman prepares a *Job Timecard* (exhibit 9) for each worker who will do any part of the job. Every time the operator starts or stops work on the job, the employee has his or her card time-stamped. When the employee finishes the job, the card is time-stamped again and completed.

The Job Timecards provide information for preparing the operator's paycheck.

Exhibit 8.—Job-cost record for a nondepartmentalized plant

JOB COST RECORD

FOR _____ ORDER NO. _____

PRODUCT _____ QUANTITY _____

DATE WANTED _____ DATE STARTED _____ DATE COMPLETED _____

DIRECT MATERIALS			DIRECT LABOR			APPLIED OVERHEAD		
DATE	REQ. NO.	AMOUNT	DATE	TIME CARD NO.	AMOUNT	BASIS	RATE	AMOUNT

SUMMARY FOR ORDER NO. _____

DIRECT MATERIALS _____

DIRECT LABOR _____

APPLIED OVERHEAD _____

TOTAL FACTORY COST _____

FACTORY COST PER UNIT _____

5. A cost clerk collects the Job Timecards daily or weekly. The clerk figures the labor costs and sorts the cards by production orders. Then the clerk records the direct-labor costs on the Job Cost Record for each job on which work has been done. Some production orders may require days or even weeks in one department. When that is the case, daily job timecards may be needed to keep the Job Cost Records current.

Exhibit 9.—Job timecard

JOB TIME CARD							
NAME _____ CARD NO. ____							
DEPARTMENT_____ CLOCK NO. ____							
DATE	PROD'N ORDER NO	MACHINE NO.	TIME STARTED	TIME STOPPED	TOTAL HOURS	WAGE RATE	TOTAL COST
NO. OF PIECES FINISHED_____ APPROVED BY_____							

6. The *Cost of Overhead* includes all manufacturing costs except direct materials and direct labor. These costs cannot be assigned to or identified with individual jobs, so they are *applied* to jobs on the basis of so much per direct labor hour or machine hour, or on some other basis.

7. Once the method for distributing overhead cost has been decided, the overhead cost can be calculated for each job and entered on the Job Cost Record. The Job Cost Records should show the overhead rate and basis used as well as the amount applied to the job.

8. On any date, the *Job Cost Record* (exhibits 7 and 8) for a given job shows all the costs of the job—direct materials, direct labor, and overhead applied—as of that date. All the job cost records together make up a subsidiary, or special, ledger called the cost ledger.

These costs are entered also in the Work-in-Process account in the general ledger. The accounting entries here are usually monthly totals from the materials requisitions, job time cards, and overhead application calculations. The Work-in-Process account is called a *control account* because its balance is always equal to the total of all costs of *uncompleted jobs* in the cost ledger.

In some cases, it may be more convenient to use three work-in-process accounts—Material-in-Process, Labor-in-Process, and Overhead-in-Process—than to put all costs into a single account. But no matter how many work-in-process accounts are used, the principle is the same: When all accounting entries have been made, the total of the costs shown on the uncompleted job-cost records should equal the total costs in the work-in-process account(s).

The job-cost records are the hub of any cost system for a jobbing plant. The entries made on these forms are the end result of all the procedures used to gather cost details.

Just what type of job-cost records will be used depends on a number of factors—the number of types of raw materials and component parts used; the length of time required to complete each job; the number of employees doing direct labor on each job; the basis for applying overhead; the number of different overhead rates (for different operations); the degree to which the factory is departmentalized; and any special production or accounting techniques used.

The fundamental requirements, however, are always the same. There must be space for job identification; for periodic entries of direct material, direct labor, and overhead costs; and for a summary of total costs. Exhibits 7 and 8 (pages 162–163) show typical job-cost record forms for departmentalized and nondepartmentalized plants.

9. When a job is finished, entries are made on the Production Control Record (exhibit 2,) and on a monthly *Pro-*

duction Cost Summary similar to the one shown as exhibit 10. The data for the Production Cost Summary are taken from the summary section of the Job Cost Record. This report is a useful source of end-result cost information for the management of a manufacturing business.

10. At the end of each month or whatever period fits the cycle of manufacturing activity, the total costs of all completed jobs, as shown on the monthly Production Cost Summary, are entered in the journal. This journal entry transfers costs from the. Work-in-Process account to the Finished-Product Inventory account:

                                            Debit   Credit

Finished product inventory xxx
   Work in process xxx
To transfer costs of completed jobs to finished product inventory.

11. When finished products are sold to a customer, either on special order or out of inventory, the costs of those products are

Exhibit 10.—Production cost summary

DATE COMPL.	ORDER NO.	PRODUCT	QUANTITY	DIRECT MATERIALS	DIRECT LABOR	APPLIED OVERH'D	TOTAL COST	COST PER UNIT

PRODUCTION COST SUMMARY FOR MONTH OF _____
FOR DEPARTMENT _____

taken out of the inventory account and charged to the Cost of Goods Sold account. (The Cost of Goods Sold will appear in the income statement.)

	Debit	Credit
Cost of goods sold	xxx	
Finished product inventory		xxx

To record the sale of products.

. This chapter has outlined the basic steps in a cost-accounting system for a jobbing plant. No matter how complex the manufacturing operation, a cost system must embody these same techniques, expanded or adapted to meet the specific needs of the management.